COLD LIGHT

Creatures, Discoveries, and Inventions That Glow

Anita Sitarski

BOYDS MILLS PRESS
Honesdale, Pennsylvania

To Karol, my own very cool light, who makes me better than I am
—A.S.

A very special thanks is due to Dr. Steven Haddock, Monterey Bay Aquarium Research Institute. His outstanding images, generosity, and patience are at the heart of this book. An additional special thanks goes to Dr. Aladar Szalay, president of the International Society for Bioluminescence and Chemiluminescence, for reading the entire manuscript and offering invaluable assistance.

The following people have offered their generosity of time and spirit to a stranger, leading to the realization of this book:

Dr. Bruce Applegate, Purdue University; Dr. Mario Baraldini, University of Bologna; Dr. Bruce Bryan, Prolume, Ltd.; Dr. Martin Chalfie, Columbia University; Dr. Charles Chester, Spring Hill College; Dr. Christopher Contag, Stanford University; Charlene Cooper, AntiCancer, Inc.; Peg Dirckx, Montana State University at Bozeman; Alan Guisewite, Carnegie Mellon University; Dr. Paul Hebert, Biodiversity Institute of Ontario; Dr. Robert M. Hoffman, AntiCancer, Inc.; Dr. Stephen Howell, Iowa State University; Dr. Michael Latz, University of California, San Diego; Piotr Madanecki, Medical University of Gdańsk; Garry Maguire, Springbrook Research Centre; Jan Meerman, biological-diversity.info; Dr. Shuji Nakamura, University of California, Santa Barbara; Prof. Aldo Roda, University of Bologna; Dr. Philip E. Stanley, Cambridge Research and Technology Transfer Ltd.; and Dr. Tony Yu, Genelux Corporation.

Thanks to my editor, Andy Boyles, for guidance and patience with a newbie. Thanks to Katie Bunker for helping to pull off a few miracles. Thanks also to my husband, Michael Sitarski, for determination and a tripod, and my son, Kevin Sitarski, for a fellow writer's perspective and research assistance.

Picture Credits

Contents

Introduction 5

1 How Can You Be So Cold?
The Stone That Captured the Sun 7

2 Back Off, I Need Some Air
The Chicken That Glowed in the Dark 11

3 What's in a Name?
The Inside Story of Fire Beetles and Glowing Mushrooms 16

4 They're Everywhere
Shedding Light on Bioluminescent Creatures 20

5 Don't Bother Me, I'm Busy
The Secret Lives of Glowing Sea Creatures 23

6 You Light Up My Life
Those Special Fireflies 28

7 Send In the Clones
New Frontiers in Bioluminescence Research 32

8 I Don't Need You Anymore
Jellyfish GFP and Beyond 37

9 New Kids on the Block
Man-Made Cool Light 41

Epilogue 44

To Learn More 45

Glossary 46

Index 47

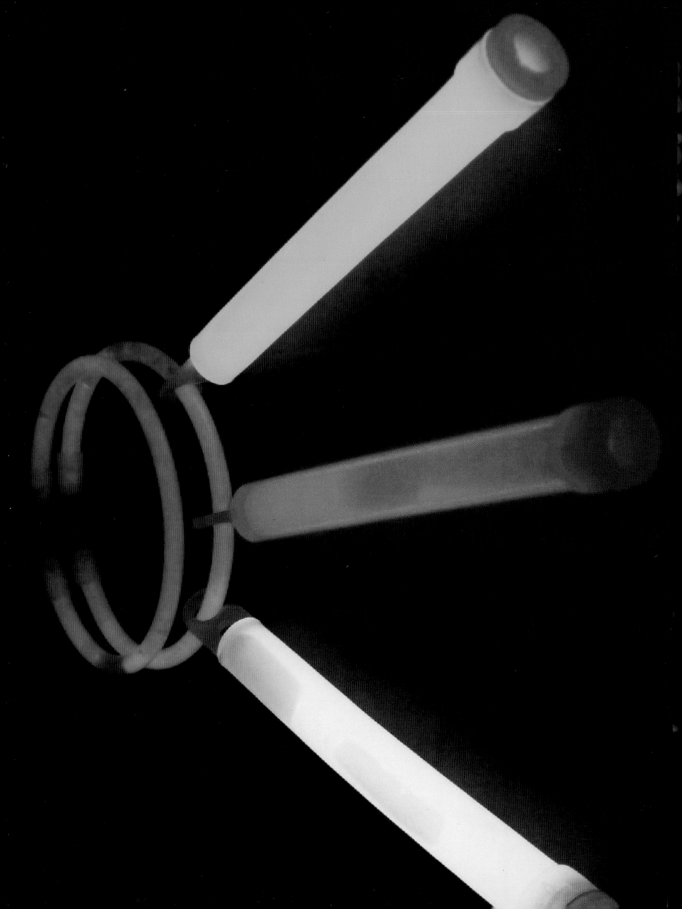

Introduction

What a Reaction!

Light Sticks and Other Cool Light

*S*NAP!
HAVE YOU EVER USED a light stick? Then you are familiar with the snap that gets the glow to go. Ever wonder just what that snap does?

The center of a light stick holds a delicate glass tube. This capsule most often contains a chemical that you may have seen in your home medicine cabinet—hydrogen peroxide. (Some people use it to clean cuts or even to bleach their hair.) The rest of the light stick contains a second chemical and a dye that glows a certain color when it receives energy.

When you bend the light stick until you feel that snap, you are breaking the glass tube and releasing the hydrogen peroxide solution into the second chemical. Shaking the tube speeds up the mixing of the two, which act on each other to make new chemicals. This reaction produces energy that causes the dye to glow. Different dyes are used to produce different colored light sticks, or glow sticks, as they are also called.

One of the cool things about glow sticks is that they're, well, cool. That is, the reaction produces light and very little heat. Scientists call light produced at low temperatures luminescence (loo-muh-NES-ens). The *lumin* part means "light." When luminescence is caused by a chemical reaction, like in a glow stick, it's called chemiluminescence.

The knowledge needed to produce glow sticks came from studies of fireflies—the champions of cold light. Since *bio* means "life," when scientists talk about chemiluminescence that takes place in living things like fireflies, they call it bioluminescence. (Yes, it's another huge word—just be glad it's not "biochemiluminescence"!) A third kind of cold light can be seen in things like glow-in-the-dark stickers and toys. This type also has a long name, but perhaps we'll wait until later for that.

New discoveries about how cold light works and how to use it are being made practically every day. People are even investigating entirely new ways to produce cold light. This is definitely a cool time to take a new look at the fascinating story of cold light. It's a story that's a lot like a relay race. Discoveries made by one scientist are passed like a baton to the next researcher and the next, each one adding to our understanding of cold light. This is their story, and it's cool.

Light sticks are cool in more ways than one. They produce cold light created by chemicals, a process called chemiluminescence.

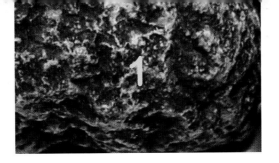

How Can You Be So Cold?

The Stone That Captured the Sun

So, WHAT'S THE BIG DEAL about cold light? Ever since human beings discovered how to make fire, we've been able to produce our own light. Our light has always been the result of heating something until it gets so hot that it glows. Believe it or not, even the standard electric light bulb works on the same basic idea as a caveman's fire. Instead of dead tree branches, of course, a light bulb contains a thin wire, or filament. Electricity makes the filament so hot that it gives off light, but the energy it gives off is still mostly heat. (Light produced by extreme heat is called incandescence.)

All light, hot or cold, is produced the same way. It starts with the tiny parts that make up all things—atoms. One of the simplest ways to think of each atom is as a miniature solar system, much too small to be seen. Instead of a sun, the center of an atom is the nucleus. Instead of planets, the nucleus is orbited by small particles called electrons. Like the planets, the electrons follow an orbit at a particular distance from the nucleus. Unlike the planets, electrons may share orbits with other electrons.

The electrons can absorb energy and jump to higher orbits, farther away from the nucleus. The party doesn't last forever,

Ouch! Light-bulb filaments are hot stuff! Incandescence produces some light, but mostly heat.

though. The electrons wind up dropping back to their original orbits. When this happens, they send out the extra energy that was boosting them higher. We see this energy as light.

Electrons can be energized by heat (moving atoms or molecules), like in a standard light bulb. The energy from the electricity that goes through that light bulb comes out as about 90% heat and only 10% light. Electrons can also be directly energized by a chemical reaction (light sticks, fireflies) or even by light (glow-in-the-dark toys). Almost 100% of a firefly's excess energy is in the form of light.

People didn't really begin to study nature's cold lights until 1602. That was the year that Vincenzo Casciarolo found a mysterious rock. Vincenzo didn't set out to study luminescence. He was a shoemaker in Bologna, Italy, whose hobby was alchemy—trying to make gold using other minerals. Many edu-

Bologna Stone (barium sulfate) rocked the cold-light world.

cated men were searching for a way to make a "philosopher's stone" that could be used to make gold. (This was a "science" taken very seriously in those days, although we know now that it was not possible.) One day, Vincenzo found an unusual-looking rock on Monte Paderno, just outside of Bologna. It looked like a good candidate for making gold, so Vincenzo took it home and started working with it. He used the same procedures as most alchemists. He ground part of the stone into a powder and heated it in a fire. Alas, poor Vincenzo never did make gold from this stone. However, he did find that, after the grinding and heating, the stone seemed to have a magical ability. It "absorbed" light when he put it in the sun and gave light back in the darkness. Sometimes, he mixed the powdered stone with water or egg white and shaped it into animals before heating it. So, you might say that Vincenzo Casciarolo made the first fun glow-in-the-dark objects.

More importantly, he showed his stone to many educated people in Italy. It set off a great debate in that country and elsewhere. In a way, all the wonderful things we've come to understand today about luminescence started with Vincenzo's *lapis solaris*—his "sun rock."

The material that was discovered in the Bologna Stone gives off light for the same reason as the material in a firefly—

Phosphors—The Reason Cold Light Lights

Today, we know the Bologna Stone is barite, or barium sulfate. The Bologna Stone and other materials that are able to give off light when their atoms are excited are called phosphors (FOS-ferz). Phosphors are involved in all kinds of cold light, so you might also hear luminescence referred to as phosphorescence (FOS-fer-es-ens).

Phosphors are all around us. For instance, many TV screens or computer monitors are coated inside with phosphors that can give off three different colors—red, green, and blue. An electron beam excites them. In fluorescent lights, phosphors give off visible light when their electrons get excited by ultraviolet light, which is a kind of light that humans can't see.

its electrons get excited by an outside energy source and then calm down, sending out their extra energy as light. The difference is that the outside energy source for the stone was another light, not a chemical reaction. Since "photo" means "light," like what you need to make a *photo*graph, this kind of luminescence can be called "*photo*-luminescence." Often, this type of cold light is called fluorescence (flor-ES-ens).

We've come a long way since Vincenzo Casciarolo's time, but his glow-in-the-dark rock started people wondering again about all of nature's cold lights. It started a lot of thought about bioluminescence (BI-o-loo-muh-NES-ens), cold light produced by living creatures. The next scientist to grab the research baton and run with it was the father of modern chemistry, Robert Boyle.

These glow-in-the-dark stickers are photoluminescent. An outside light source excites their electrons, and the stickers continue glowing after the light goes out. They're fun, and a lot safer than hanging pieces of the Bologna Stone from the ceiling!

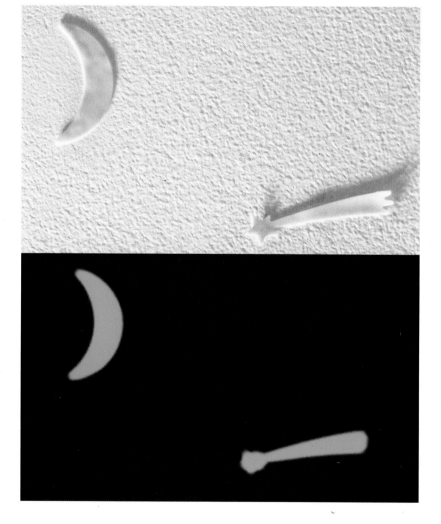

2

Back Off, I Need Some Air

The Chicken That Glowed in the Dark

IN 1667, A FAMOUS CHEMIST named Robert Boyle was the first to study bioluminescence scientifically. He was interested in alchemy just as Vincenzo Casciarolo had been, but he did plenty of other experiments as well. One night, one of Robert Boyle's servants called for him to come see something extraordinary in the pantry. There on a pantry shelf, Robert Boyle found some chicken that had been bought about a week before. (No refrigerators in those days!) The meat was covered with about twenty spots of various sizes glowing with a greenish blue light. Boyle would later write that when it was picked up, the movement caused the meat to glow even more brightly, putting on a "rather splendid show."

Boyle did several experiments with this meat. One of them involved eating some of the meat! I'm happy to say he survived, because he also did a rather famous experiment with the glowing meat and other glowing things, such as mushrooms. Boyle had invented a way to pump all the air out of a glass jar. When he put glowing specimens in the jar and pumped out all the air, he found that their light went out. When he

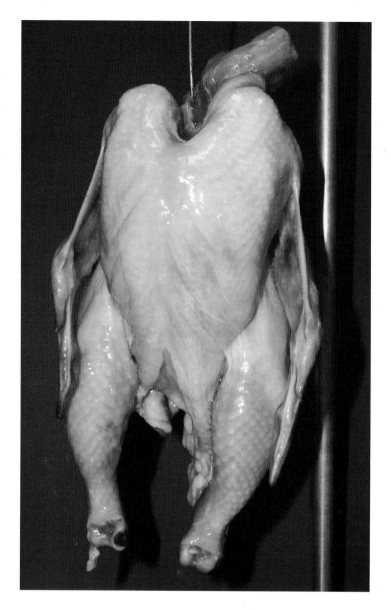

Inspired by Robert Boyle and his encounter with glowing chicken, Nathan Bright and Dr. Bruce Applegate at Purdue University covered this chicken with the same bioluminescent bacteria. The photo is a bright spot in talks about food safety.

let the air back in again, the glow resumed. He had discovered that bioluminescence needs air to work. We now know that it's the oxygen part of air that is needed for the chemical reaction to take place.

But what was causing the meat to glow in the first place? That would be the smallest of bioluminescent creatures, bacteria. These microscopic organisms show up in surprising places, from chicken or fish that's been left out on the counter too long to the pouches under the eyes of flashlight

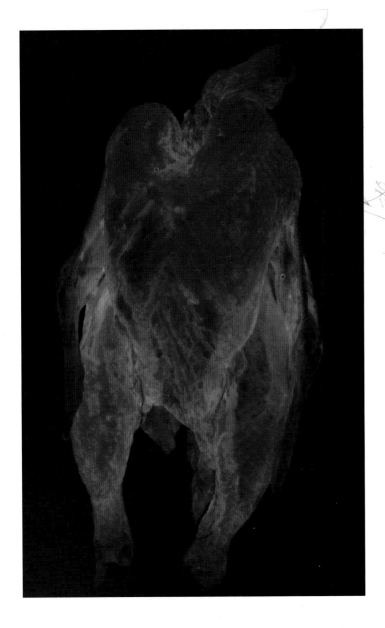

fish in the sea. Luckily for Robert Boyle, the greenish bioluminescent bacteria that show up in spoiling meat signal that other harmful bacteria may also be present or are coming soon, but the glowing stuff is not harmful in itself.

Besides signaling that meat is spoiling, bioluminescent bacteria have been useful in other ways. Before the use of bacteria-killers like antiseptics, luminescent bacteria could often be seen as a dull glow in the wounds of patients. Long after Boyle's experiments,

Bacterial Math

The glow from bioluminescent bacteria can be seen because they multiply quickly and grow in huge numbers. At the International Exhibition in Paris in 1900, a scientist filled jars with glowing bacteria and placed them around a room. The light from all the bacteria was so bright that people could read by it and even recognize faces of people twenty feet away. How many bacteria were needed to produce this effect? Millions and millions. It would take 100,000,000,000,000,000,000 (100 quintillion) bacteria to equal the light from a 60-watt light bulb. The light at the International Exhibition was not nearly this bright, but you get the idea.

Bioluminescent bacteria growing in a prepared liquid solution. The center is frothy because the liquid is being stirred. What would stirring do?

The same solution in the dark. Stirring helps keep oxygen in the solution. Without it, the glow fades quickly.

doctors working on wounded soldiers during the American Civil War, in the 1860s, reported that the patients with glowing wounds often healed better. It is thought that the bioluminescent bacteria causing the glow helped to remove dead tissue that might have otherwise supported disease-causing germs. You might say that these patients had a "healthy glow" about them.

Today, we can check for pollution using certain kinds of marine (ocean) bacteria that lose their glow in the presence of toxic (poisonous) chemicals in water or soil. These bacteria can be freeze-dried, like some instant coffee crystals, or used fresh in detectors that measure their light. Robert Boyle, of course, had no idea what he started when he cut off the air supply to his glowing specimens. We, however, get to see what was around the bend.

Bacterial Art

For Earth Day in 2002, students at Montana State University at Bozeman produced a week-long art exhibit in a darkened gallery. The students "painted" their artworks using special marine bacteria that start to glow only when there are large numbers of them in one place. The students prepared flat covered dishes with nutrients needed to grow the bacteria and created designs in the dishes with solutions containing the bacteria. At first, the designs were invisible. As the bacteria colonies grew, they gave off a blue light and the designs could be seen. Over the course of a week, the bacterial artwork grew brighter and brighter and then started to fade as the food in the dishes was used up and the bacteria died.

This de-LIGHT-ful art gallery at Montana State University at Bozeman really gave bacteria a chance to shine.

3

What's in a Name?

The Inside Story of Fire Beetles and Glowing Mushrooms

ACTUALLY, WHAT WAS around the bend was about two hundred years of nothing. Oh, sure, people still talked about cold light. They even used cold light as they had for centuries. Some people living near oceans smeared jellyfish goo on branches to produce cold torches to light their way on a dark beach. During the seventeenth century, farmers in Sweden made use of wood infected with glowing fungi, or fox fire, to light haylofts. This was much better than candles or lanterns because the cold light of fox fire would not accidentally set the hay on fire. In the New World, brilliant Jamaican fire beetles were put in cages to light homes and were even worn by women as hair ornaments.

However, it wasn't until 1885 that the next big hurdle in bioluminescent research was jumped. It was then that a French scientist named Raphael Dubois did a very creative experiment using the fire beetle (*Pyrophorus*). Dubois removed the parts of the beetle that make light. He ground up these light organs and mixed some with cold water. The cold-water mixture glowed for a while and then went out. Dubois decided that whatever was making the light had been used up. Then he added some ground-up light organs to hot water. This mixture did not glow at all—even after the water had cooled. He decided that the heat of the water must have destroyed something needed to make

Those Fun Guys, the Fungi

Fungi are organisms so strange that they need their own kingdom, separate from both plants and animals. Some fungi are tiny, like yeast and mold. Others are larger, with caps and stems. You know those fungi as mushrooms. (One mushroom is the fruit body of a fungus.)

Not all fungi glow, but those that do usually have an eerie reputation. There are many stories of "magical" fox fire, the name given to the pale greenish glow that can be seen on dead or rotting tree trunks and branches, but it's just caused by glowing fungi that attach themselves to the wood to feed on it. If insects and animals are attracted to a fungus by its light, they spread its spores in a wide area after eating it. In this way, the fungus might "pass the torch" to whole new generations.

Fun guys? It looks as if they're ready for a party, but these bioluminescent mushrooms are probably just trying to attract attention from any passerby that can spread their spores.

I Always Knew
You Were Bright

The brightest bioluminescent insect belongs to a family of beetles called Elateridae (el-la-TARE-re-dee), or click beetles. Click beetles that light up are known as fire beetles. The brightest known bioluminescent land animal is a fire beetle called . . . (tah dah!) . . . Pyrophorus noctilucus. Fortunately, they are also known as Jamaican click beetles or "cucujo" beetles. These large beetles (almost 2 inches long) emit a light so bright that you could read by it if you held the cucujo close enough to what you were reading. Luckily for purposes such as reading by beetle, fire beetles emit a steady glow rather than flashing on and off as fireflies do. The beetles use their light mostly for finding mates. None of them have been spotted reading by their own light.

No, those aren't headlights. They're the light organs on a Pyrophorus noctilucus—*cucujo beetle to its friends.*

This cucujo was photographed using its own light. About forty of these guys would give off as much light as a candle.

light. Finally, Dubois mixed his cold-water solution with the now-cooled hot-water solution. It glowed!

Dubois repeated this experiment many times with other glowing animals and fungi. He began to realize that he was dealing with at least two other things besides oxygen. One substance had been used up in the cold. One had been destroyed by heat. When they were mixed together, the substance in the cold water that had not been destroyed interacted with a still-unused, heat-resistant substance in the formerly hot water. That was why they made light again. Dubois named the chemical that was not affected by heat luciferin (loo-SIF-er-in). *Lucifer* means "light bearer" in Latin. Dubois named the chemical that was destroyed by heat luciferase (loo-SIF-er-ASE). The *–ase* ending showed that this was a special kind of chemical called an enzyme. He knew that enzymes are easily destroyed by heat.

Dubois made some brilliant conclusions based on this experiment. Scientists today still refer to luciferin and luciferase. So, by the end of the nineteenth century, thanks to Robert Boyle and Raphael Dubois, it was known that a huge variety of glowing creatures are lit up by a chemical reaction between luciferin and luciferase when oxygen is present. DuBois also spread his interest by sending some luminescent material to E. Newton Harvey, an American biologist who eventually became known as the Dean of Bioluminescence. Dr. Harvey spent forty years studying bioluminescent organisms, describing and classifying every one then known. Cold light research was finally starting to heat up.

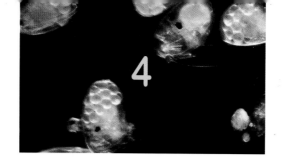

4

They're Everywhere

Shedding Light on Bioluminescent Creatures

EDMUND NEWTON HARVEY was enthusiastic about all sciences, but especially biology, from the time he was a boy. As a student and later as a professor at Princeton University, he was able to travel all over the world studying its creatures. In 1909, he took an exotic trip on a small ship to work at Dry Tortugas Marine Biological Laboratory near Key West, Florida. From the dark ship deck, E. Newton Harvey had spectacular views of glowing seawater stimulated by the moving ship. This glowing water is an example of bioluminescence because it's not the water that's glowing. It's millions of tiny biolu-

minescent creatures called dinoflagellates (DI-no-FLA-jel-lates). The sight of so much bioluminescence couldn't help but interest the naturally curious Harvey.

Each dinoflagellate is made of only a single cell. Many dinoflagellates have characteristics of both plants and animals, and several kinds are bioluminescent. They are found near the surface and are especially plentiful in late summer—a lot like the algae in swimming pools and ponds. Millions of them together make enough light to be visible—sometimes even enough light to read by. When they really get going, there can be as many as several million dinoflagellates in a liter of seawater—quite a sight! If Harvey had jumped into the water, he would have come out glowing like a ghost from all the dinoflagellates clinging to him.

Soon after this eye-opening experience with bioluminescence, Harvey went on a study trip to the Great Barrier Reef in Australia. After seeing more biolumines-cent seas and collecting many luminescent sea creatures, Harvey knew he had found his life's work.

Unfortunately, it's not easy to see the light from most marine creatures, such as dinoflagellates, when they're studied in a laboratory. They also are difficult to keep alive. In 1916, Harvey found a solution to this problem in Japan. There he studied ostracods. These tiny creatures are related to shrimps but have clear clamlike shells.

One type of ostracod called *Vargula hilgendorfii* grows and glows in shallow water off the coast of Japan. It shoots bright blue clouds of light into the water to protect itself from predators. When the bodies of these ostracods are collected and dried, they produce a blue glow when mixed with water, even if they've been stored for twenty years or more. This property made them perfect creatures for Harvey to use while trying to learn more about how bioluminescence works.

Many kilograms of dried *Vargula* (called by a different name, *Cypridina,* back then) were shipped from Japan to Harvey at Princeton over the next forty years.

He also studied bioluminescence in as many other creatures as he could, including Japanese and American fireflies, fire beetles, jellyfish, bacteria, and various deep-sea fish.

How I Wonder Why You Glow

Okay—so they're cool, but why do dinoflagellates glow? What's in it for them? Dinoflagellates can be eaten by any number of small sea creatures. To use an example, one of these small creatures is called a copepod. When the dinoflagellates are disturbed by one of these predators out looking for food, they give a bright flash. The light can attract a fish that is interested in eating the copepod. At the very least, the dinoflagellate-eating predator is often scared away. It makes sense that this method of defense is called a "burglar alarm."

Harvey made an interesting discovery about luciferin and luciferase, the chemicals that combine to produce the light. While every bioluminescent creature he studied appeared to have these two substances, he found that each creature had its own types. The luciferin from a firefly, for instance, will not light up if mixed with the luciferase from a jellyfish. Now scientists know of dozens of types of luciferins and luciferases, but only a few have been completely studied.

Around the time that Harvey was studying all the bioluminescent organisms he could find, an American scientist and explorer named William Beebe was making it possible to see deep-sea luminescent creatures in their own habitats. Between the two men, our knowledge of glowing creatures increased at breathtaking speed.

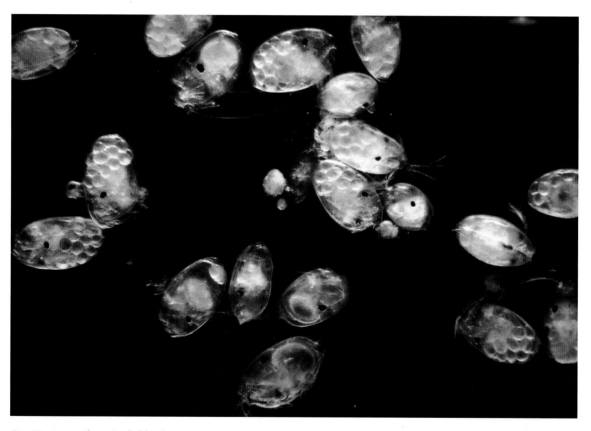

Dr. Harvey used ostracods like these. So did Japanese soldiers in World War II. The soldiers mixed dried ostracod powder with water and smeared some on themselves. The blue glow helped them locate each other in the dark.

5

Don't Bother Me, I'm Busy

The Secret Lives of Glowing Sea Creatures

THE OCEAN is bursting with bioluminescence. In 1934, while Harvey was studying how bioluminescence works, William Beebe and Otis Barton descended to a depth over half a mile (923 meters) beneath the ocean surface. A ship on the surface lowered them by cable in a device called a bathysphere (BATH-es-fere). Beebe and Barton had invented and built this bathysphere, which was basically a hollow metal globe with observation windows. More than 80% of the creatures that live at the depths they explored, 200 to nearly 1,000 meters below the ocean surface, are bioluminescent. Beebe found himself overwhelmed when he tried to observe and record all that he saw.

He wrote of the adventure: "Over two hours had passed since we left the deck and I knew that the nerves of both my staff and myself were getting ragged with constant tenseness and strain. My eyes were weary with the flashing of eternal lights. . . . So I asked for our ascent."

On that historic first dive, Beebe described creatures with "pale yellow and pale bluish" lights. The ocean also contains living lights in shades of green and red. However, the most common color for bioluminescence in the ocean is blue or

*Now you see him . . .
This small squid in the
genus* Abraliopsis *has bean-
shaped photophores as well
as small light organs that
cover its underside.*

blue-white. Why? Blue light travels the farthest through seawater. So, if you're an ocean creature who wants to see or be seen, blue light is always in fashion.

Lots of fish at this depth use their lights to hide in plain sight. Many squid, including the small *Abraliopsis*, rise nearer to the surface to feed at night. Light from photophores, light-making organs, across the squid's underside help to hide it. Predators below see scattered lights that blend with the filtered light from above instead of a definite outline of the squid.

Pearly white light organs on the snouts and undersides of lantern fish also help them hide from predators below them.

The lantern fish use their lights for other reasons as well. They have two white headlights that send out a beam more than a foot long. Curious prey that are attracted to the bright lights are goners. Also, there are more than 220 kinds of lantern fish, each with its own arrangement of light organs all over its body. Lantern fish can use the special light patterns to identify their own species and find mates.

. . . Now you don't!
If you were a predator fish down below, those dots of light would look just like moonlight
reflecting off the water. For the squid, that's better than having its body block out the moonlight
(a dead, you should pardon the expression, giveaway).

How special! Only other dragonfish will be able to spot the reddish light under this guy's eye.

The anglerfish solves the problem of finding a mate in the dark in a different way. Some female anglers can be as long as 36 inches, but those males reach only about 6 inches. Males permanently attach themselves to the females, hooking right into their bloodstream to receive nutrients. The female has a fishing pole that grows out of her head. It ends in a bulb filled with bioluminescent bacteria. Smaller fish are attracted to this lighted lure, providing food for the female and her (very) attached mate.

Dragonfish use their lights to find one another and to fool their enemies, but with a little twist. Like many others, dragonfish have lights along their sides that confuse enemies into not seeing their large black shapes. However, some dragonfish also have a red headlight beneath each eye. They are the only fish to make red light. Remember, blue travels the best underwater. Only other dragonfish have the ability to see this red light. It's like a secret code that lets them see one another without being seen by others.

Not all bioluminescence actually stays on the creature using it. Some deep-sea squid fool their enemies by squirting light-making chemicals into the water. They then disappear in a cloud of blue-green light. Jellyfish and some shrimp also prefer to defend themselves with a blinding cloud of light. This was also some of the light that so dazzled Beebe in the ocean's depths.

Whether they're attracting mates, finding and attracting prey, or avoiding being eaten, all marine creatures use one of two general types of light systems. Some, like flashlight fish, carry bioluminescent bacteria. Most make their own light much as fireflies do. These light-producers, like hatchet fish and jellyfish, have elaborate structures for producing and displaying their light. The hatchet fish, for example, has light-producing (photogenic) tissue, pigment, color filters, lenses, and reflectors. If it sounds complicated, it is. At least, researchers have been kept busy since the 1600s trying to learn all they can about cold light and the creatures that make it.

After Harvey and Beebe quickened the pace, the person to run the next lap on this race for knowledge was a man who had been one of Harvey's students at Princeton, William McElroy.

This particular anglerfish, Chaenophryne longiceps, *may look big and scary but is actually about 1 1/2 inches (4 centimeters) long. Although most bioluminescent sea creatures make their own light, the anglerfish carries around glowing bacteria in that lure growing out of her head.*

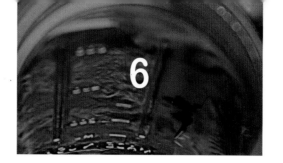

You Light Up My Life

ALOT HAD BEEN LEARNED about bioluminescence in a short time, but no real uses were found for this knowledge until the 1940s. That's when Dr. William McElroy started studying fireflies. He'd been guided by the famous E. Newton Harvey while studying at Princeton. A short time later, he was a professor himself at Johns Hopkins University. Fireflies were plentiful on the campus, and it was a natural step for him to study their bioluminescence. Dr. McElroy knew about a substance found in all living cells that is called ATP (adenosine triphosphate), which works as an energy transfer system. It helps cells change stored energy to usable energy. Since light is a form of energy, it made sense for Dr. McElroy to investigate the effects of ATP on bioluminescence. McElroy found that adding ATP to ground fireflies caused a brilliant flash of light to appear. The more ATP he added, the longer the flash lasted.

Here, then, is how the process is now described. The firefly's light is the result of a chemical reaction between oxygen, ATP, and luciferin. The enzyme luciferase is not changed or used up in the reaction, but it must be there for the

What a bright idea! Fireflies have been "amazing terrific partners" in the study of cold light, in large part because of their connection to ATP (which really stands for adenosine triphosphate).

reaction to take place. It is known as a catalyst. After McElroy, scientists found that magnesium was also necessary for the reaction.

McElroy's discovery of the ATP connection to firefly light suddenly gave the process of bioluminescence practical uses. Since ATP is found only in living cells, bioluminescence can now be used to detect unseen living organisms.

Firefly chemicals are used to detect the presence of bacteria in drinking water, milk, or in food-processing plants. In the medical field, firefly chemicals can detect unwanted bacteria in blood or urine. They can also be used to see if certain medicines are killing enough bacteria. It has even been suggested that firefly chemicals would be useful in detecting evidence of microscopic life on Mars or other planets.

If you took a flashlight into a field of fireflies and blinked the right code, you might get some of them to land on you. Then you'd have a closeup view of those glowing abdomens.

What Did You Say Your Name Is?

First of all, the truth must be told—fireflies have nothing to do with flies. Yes, most of them do fly, but they are soft-bodied beetles, not flies. As a matter of fact, they belong to a special family of beetles known as Lampyridae (lamp—get it?).

From Kansas to New York to Florida, firefly hunters are most likely to grab the firefly Photinus pyralis *(genus—*Photinus, *species—*pyralis). *This insect is sometimes called the "Big Dipper" firefly. Unfortunately, there aren't many common names for firefly species. However, the scientific names can be fun to "translate." For example, some genus names include* Microphotus *(small light),* Pyrogaster *(fire stomach), and* Pyropyga *(fire rump).*

Just as Beebe's observations led us to learn more about how bioluminescent ocean creatures use their lights, McElroy's research increased interest in how fireflies use their light. We know that there's a kind of firefly "code" that other fireflies recognize. Different species have different codes—the number of times they flash in a row, the length of the flashes, the time they wait between their flashes, and even the pattern and height of their flight. The colors of firefly light can range from yellow to amber to green. Even the same firefly might have different flashes for different purposes. The most frequent use that fireflies make of their codes is to help them find mates.

Like many bioluminescent marine creatures, fireflies also use light as a defense. Fireflies under stress will blink a code as a warning to other fireflies. A firefly's light also serves as a warning to predators. The chemicals that make a firefly's light have a bitter taste. Birds know this and don't like to eat fireflies. This is not exactly a foolproof system of defense, however. Some predator insects have been observed eating fireflies by starting at their heads and working backward. When a predator gets to the end where the chemicals are, the abdomen, the predator drops it. This is not much consolation to the firefly at that point.

If you were to take a closer look at that discarded abdomen, you would see the photophore, the light-making organ. It contains special light-making cells. These are called photocytes (FOE-toe-sites). They are very close to the surface, just behind a transparent "window" made of a cuticle. The photocytes secrete luciferin, the light-making chemical. Behind the light-making cells are sheets of fine crystals that reflect the light, directing it through the window.

These complicated little fireflies continued to keep scientists directed in their search for ways to use bioluminescence during many years to come.

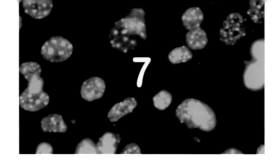

7

Send In the Clones

New Frontiers in Bioluminescence Research

WILLIAM MCELROY and his fellow scientists, including his wife, Marlene, and many of his students, were kept busy for decades building on the firefly discoveries he made in the 1940s. Between the '40s and '80s, most advances relating to firefly luciferin and luciferase could be connected in some way to Dr. McElroy. During the 1980s, he and Marlene directed work leading to the cloning of the firefly luciferase gene. This is known as the *luc* gene. Once they had the *luc* gene, researchers were able to insert it into the DNA of bacteria. When the DNA of two different organisms is com-

bined like this, it is called recombinant DNA. Bacteria can be grown easily and quickly in a laboratory. Once scientists were able to splice the *luc* gene into bacteria, they were able to grow all the firefly luciferase they needed.

They were also able to insert the firefly *luc* gene into other kinds of cells. For example, by the mid-1980s scientists at the University of California, San Diego, used recombinant DNA techniques to transfer the luciferase genes from fireflies to tobacco plants. When the plants were grown in a solution of luciferin, this resulted in leaves that glowed in the dark.

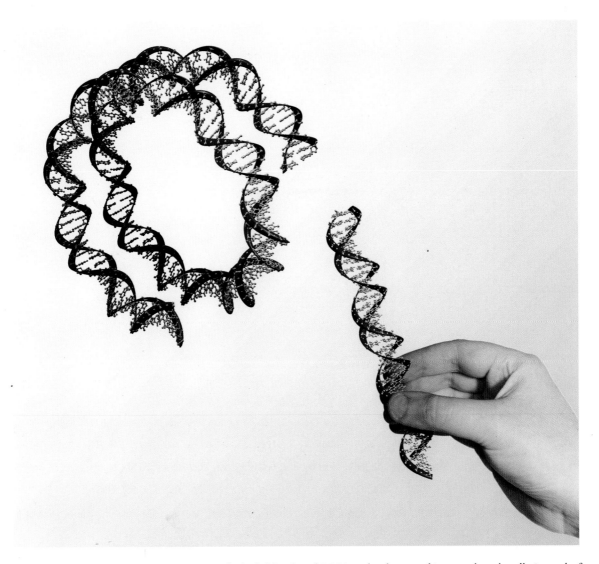

Inserting lux *genes into bacteria DNA might look like this if DNA molecules were big enough to handle instead of difficult to see even with a powerful microscope!*

Who cares? Well, researchers did this as a way of helping them figure out how hereditary information is passed from one generation to another by studying which plants inherited the glowing leaves.

Firefly genes weren't the only ones getting the recombinant DNA treatment. About the same time, scientists at Cornell University were working with cloned genes from naturally bioluminescent bacteria.

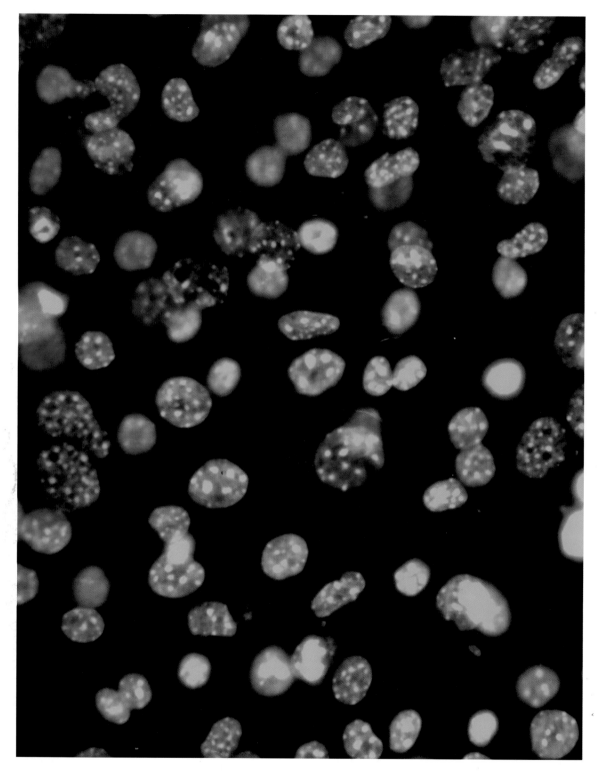

Real DNA, stained with glowing blue dye, is magnified about four hundred times using a fluorescent microscope.

The *lux* gene system, a packet of several light-producing genes, had everything needed to produce light with no need to add luciferin separately. This research team inserted *lux* genes into soybean plants in such a way that when the plants were hungry for nitrogen (which is found in fertilizer) nodules on their roots would glow. They also inserted the *lux* genes into things like worms and yeast.

Recombinant DNA, as well as *luc* and *lux* genes, opened many new uses for bioluminescence just as the discovery of the ATP connection had. For example, tracking the path of bacterial or viral infections inside the body used to be very difficult. The usual method was to infect dozens of animals, usually mice, with the disease being studied. As the infection progressed, groups of the animals were

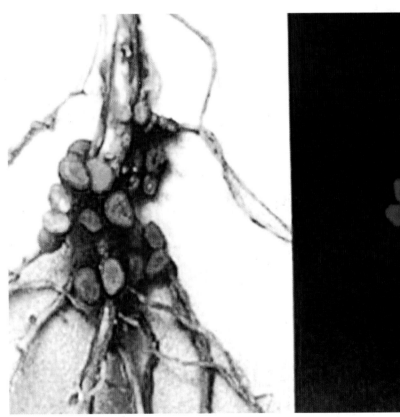

These bumps, or root nodules, grew on soybean roots because scientists added special bacteria. The nodules later glowed because the scientists had changed the bacteria by inserting lux *genes from bioluminescent bacteria.*

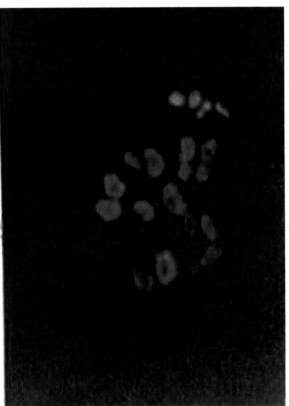

After bathing the plants in a special gas, the scientists took these photos with a camera that can detect small amounts of light.

killed and their tissues were examined to determine where and how far the disease had spread. Then two researchers named Dr. Christopher Contag and Dr. Pamela Contag began to look at bioluminescence after reading an article about detecting light that passes through tissue. They wondered if bioluminescent microorganisms inside living animals such as mice might be observed from the outside. They worked with Dr. David Benaron, who did research in medical imaging.

This Stanford University team first tested dead animal tissue by using meat from the grocery store. Dr. Pamela Contag was working with recombinant DNA to add a glow to the kind of bacteria that causes food poisoning, salmonella. Christopher buried a vial of Pamela's glowing salmonella inside a chicken breast. The light from the genetically altered salmonella came through about a half centimeter of chicken and was picked up by a sensitive light detector on the outside. Next, Christopher Contag added genes for bioluminescence to three different types of salmonella and injected them into mice. Using a digital camera, David Benaron was able to photograph the glowing bacteria that were inside the mice. They were then able to follow the course, or progression, of each infection. They could see a difference between the three types of salmonella without killing the mice to examine their tissues.

There must be hundreds, maybe thousands, of uses for bioluminescence and chemiluminescence by now. New uses are found all the time for recombinant DNA, *luc* and *lux* genes, and the different ways to see and record luminescence in animals. Scientists have learned so much about cancer and possible cures because they can actually see how the disease behaves in animals. They have a great tool for studying how genes work. That's still not the end of the story, though. The next part of the cold light trail leads right to a delicate, transparent blob of ocean life, the jellyfish.

8

I Don't Need You Anymore

Jellyfish GFP and Beyond

WHAT DO JELLYFISH, cancer detectors, and luminescent birthday cakes have in common? They're all part of the latest wave in bioluminescence research. Jellyfish come with luciferin, luciferase, and oxygen neatly packaged together. After McElroy, the focus of study shifted from those popular fireflies to many types of bioluminescent ocean creatures, including jellyfish.

In 1998, Dr. Bruce Bryan, a surgeon, and Dr. Gene Finley, a cancer researcher, started a company named Prolume. They make and sell fun glowing items and develop new bioluminescent products for more serious uses. The fun products use the idea that some jellyfish chemicals just need contact with calcium to glow. As luck would have it, calcium can be found almost everywhere, including our own skin. By 1999, Prolume was selling glowing rocks called Alien Crystals and a squirt gun that shoots water that glows when it hits its target. The secret is in powdered jellyfish chemicals mixed with the water. When this combination hits anything with calcium, the water leaves a bright glowing mark. Prolume continued to plan for glowing cake icing, glowing drinks, glowing hair mousse, and glowing ink.

One special jellyfish:
Aequorea victoria. *The*
bluish glow is from light
reflecting off parts of the
jellyfish. This creature's own
light comes out green because
of its green fluorescent protein
(GFP). The discovery of
GFP led to many other
discoveries about and uses
for luminescence.

Some of the serious work that Prolume plans to do involves using bioluminescence genes to track cancer cells. Perhaps five or ten years into the future, surgeons may be able to spray bioluminescent chemicals where they will operate and only the cancer cells will light up. The surgeon could then be sure that all the cancer cells had been removed.

This may seem like science fiction, but scientists have already found a way to produce a glow in cells that does not need pairs of chemicals like luciferin and luciferase.

It started with a mystery. When chemicals from the crystal jellyfish *(Aequorea victoria)* were used to produce light in a test tube, the light was blue. But when the jellyfish used the same chemicals, the light came out green. The answer to the puzzle was a missing piece. Back in 1962, Dr. Osamu Shimomura reported his discovery that the crystal jellyfish carries a special protein that changes the blue light to green before it leaves the jellyfish. Scientists call this green fluorescent protein, or GFP for short. In 1992, a researcher at the Woods Hole Oceanographic Institute named Douglas Prasher identified which jellyfish gene makes this protein. Why is GFP so important? Mostly because of a discovery made by scientists at Columbia University. A man named Martin Chalfie discovered that he could get GFP to light up without any of the other jellyfish chemicals. Dr. Chalfie did in the laboratory what jellyfish do inside their bodies. After placing GFP in bacterial and worm nerve cells, he shone a blue light on the GFP—and it produced green light.

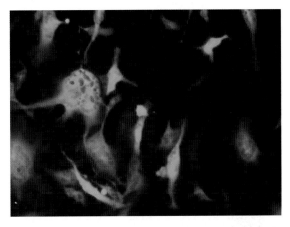

These magnified cells are glowing because they contain green fluorescent protein.

This green guy isn't a mouse from Mars. Green fluorescent protein is attached to the DNA in every cell of its body. The mouse glows green under blue light. Mice like this help with cancer and transplant research.

Never Satisfied

Yes, GFP is cool, but green light gets scattered and absorbed as it travels through living tissue. Red or infrared light, which travels about ten times farther, is better for studying bigger organisms. Two Russian biologists, Mikhail Matz and Sergey Lukyanov, were the first to come up with a red fluorescent protein. Today, many researchers rely on a brilliant red fluorescent protein called DsRed, which is cloned from a type of coral. In addition, many other colors of fluorescent proteins, suited for different research purposes, have been developed.

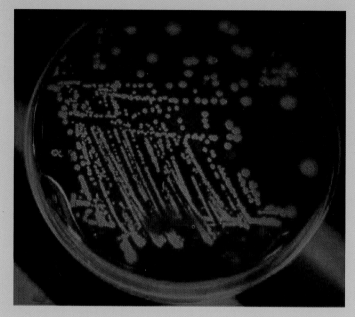

This little dish contains a lot of science. Recombinant DNA methods were used to insert the fluorescent protein DsRed into a colony of bacteria. Like GFP, DsRed lights up without luciferin or luciferase—very useful!

It's less work to get just GFP into living cells than a whole system of genes for producing a set of bioluminescent chemicals. Scientists can now add GFP to the genes of bacteria, plants, and animals, which then make their own GFP. When GFP is added to living cells, the cells can be detected simply by shining blue or ultraviolet light on them.

A protein like GFP that lights up when light is shone on it is called a fluorescent protein. Now many companies are busy producing a rainbow of fluorescent proteins for countless research purposes. Fluorescent proteins light the way in the study of how living cells work, how genes are transferred, and how diseases might be cured. And it all started with a jellyfish and a mystery.

9

New Kids on the Block

Man-Made Cool Light

SCIENTISTS have gone beyond the need to capture fireflies or jellyfish to get their glow-juice. They've moved beyond synthesized luciferin and luciferase to cloning the genes that produce them. They've even moved beyond the magic GFP to cloning genes for red-emitting proteins from coral. End of story? Nope!

Some engineers are working on a whole new source of cold light, called light-emitting diodes, or LEDs. A diode is an electronic part that allows electricity to flow in only one direction. LEDs are designed to turn that energy into light. They have a small plastic bulb around the diode to capture and focus the light that is produced. So, LEDs are not chemiluminescent—they need electricity to power them. However, unlike most electrical light sources, they don't get especially hot, and engineers are hard at work trying to eliminate what little heat they produce. With little energy wasted as heat, they are a truly cold light source.

If you've ever used a remote control, you've already used an LED. The LED inside a remote control produces a kind of light that we can't see, infrared light. But LEDs that produce visible light are all around us already. If you look carefully at newer traffic signals, you'll probably notice that instead of one light inside each round lens, there are rows and rows of tiny lights inside each circle. Those would be—you guessed it—LEDs.

Because LEDs already turn most of the energy they use into light instead of wasted heat, they use much less electricity to produce the same amount of light. Also, since they don't have filaments to burn out, they last a long time. Big cities can see huge savings in operating costs just by replacing all their old traffic lights with LEDs.

LEDs are still the babies of the cold-light world. Engineers have been hard at work on a few problems, like making

There's no stopping them! LEDs are everywhere you look.

Filament-Free and Lovin' It: The Light-Emitting Diode (LED)

Most diodes today are semiconductor chips, like those made from silicon (the main element in sand). A silicon crystal can be treated with a small impurity that makes it have extra electrons. This is N-type silicon. Another silicon crystal can be treated with a small impurity that gives it extra spaces for electrons. This is P-type silicon. If the two types of silicon, or some other semiconductor, are put together and an electric current is passed through in the right direction, excited extra electrons from the N-type will drop down into the spaces of the P-type.

The spaces in the P-type semiconductor are at a lower orbit, closer to the atom's nucleus, than the electrons in the N-type semiconductor. As each electron moves down from one orbital level to a lower one, it gives off light. If the right materials, such as gallium instead of silicon, are used with the right impurities, the extra energy left over at the end of the electron party will be given off, or emitted, as visible light. Different kinds of semiconductors will create different colors of light.

So, the movement of electrons in a semiconductor, not the heating of a filament, creates light in an LED. Rarely, an LED may also contain a phosphor to adjust the color of the light, but the production of light does not require a phosphor as it does in a fluorescent bulb. The semiconductor chip is placed inside a small plastic housing to direct the light.

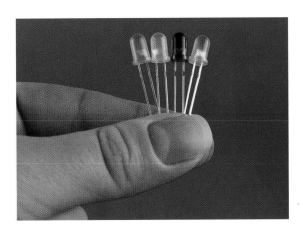

Good things come in small packages. Each LED is smaller than a thumbnail, but together they are creating a revolution in cold-light technology.

them cheaper to produce. Believe it or not, jellyfish might provide one way to make cheaper LEDs. A team of electrical engineers led by Mark Thompson at the University of Southern California was inspired by the GFP found in bioluminescent jellyfish. They created organic (based on something living) LEDs, or OLEDs. They copied GFP and used it as one of the materials in an LED. The appeal of OLEDs is that they may prove simpler and cheaper to produce than LEDs.

Another problem for LED developers was getting the light bright enough and white enough. Because of the materials used to make LEDs, colors like red and yellow were easier to produce at first. Of course, white light is the most useful for practical lighting purposes like headlights, streetlights, and home lighting. Those uses

are possible because of a man named Shuji Nakamura. In the early 1990s, he worked first to produce a blue LED. To do this, he even had to invent a process to manufacture the material he needed to produce blue light. Then Dr. Nakamura had the idea of coating the blue LED with a phosphor that would produce white light when struck by the blue light. The world's first white-light LED was produced.

Once they had white light, researchers worked at making it brighter and brighter. Some cars already have LED headlights. LED "light bulbs" are being sold to fit sockets where ordinary, hot incandescent light bulbs now fit.

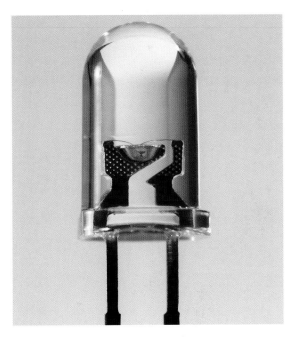

Take a close look at your future. This blue LED is about to change a big piece of our world.

Epilogue

A Very Cool Future

ALL THIS IS LEADING to a big change in your daily life—the complete replacement of the light bulb! A few years ago, this seemed like a fantasy, but now all the major lighting companies have departments doing research on LEDs. In ten or twenty years, you could have LED lighting all over your home that can be adjusted for brightness and color with the twist of a dial. Pollution will decrease because everyone will use less electricity to power their LED lights. The U.S. Department of Energy has estimated that the use of LEDs could cut national energy consumption for lighting by 29% by 2025. And eventually your grandchildren will say, "Tell us about the days when you had those really hot lights." Cool!

To Learn More

Books

Batten, Mary. *The Winking, Blinking Sea: All about Bioluminescence*. Brookfield, CT: Millbrook Press, 2000. More about bioluminescence in sea creatures such as ostracods and flashlight fish.

Collard, Sneed B., III. *A Firefly Biologist at Work*. New York: Franklin Watts, 2001. How a scientist works in the field, and lots of facts about fireflies.

Ganeri, Anita. *Creatures That Glow*. New York: Harry N. Abrams, 1995. Information about flashlight fish, fireflies, and bioluminescent fungi.

Hirschmann, Kris. *Creatures That Glow*. Creatures of the Sea. San Diego, CA: KidHaven Press, 2005. Detailed information about many glowing sea creatures and how they make use of their bioluminescence. Great photos.

Kuntz, Lynn. *Firefly*. Detroit: KidHaven Press, 2006. Detailed information and photos of fireflies around the world.

Silverstein, Alvin, and Virginia Silverstein. *Nature's Living Lights: Fireflies and Other Bioluminescent Creatures*. Boston: Little, Brown, 1988. Good description of bioluminescent insects, plants, and sea animals and how they use their light.

Easy Reading

Ashley, Susan. *Fireflies*. Milwaukee: Weekly Reader Early Learning Library, 2004. An introduction to the lives of fireflies with closeup photographs.

Barkan, Joanne. *Creatures That Glow*. New York: Doubleday, 1991. Introduces many glowing sea creatures as well as fireflies, mushrooms, and bacteria. The pictures glow in the dark.

More Challenging (High School and Above)

Pieribone, Vincent, and David F. Gruber. *Aglow in the Dark: The Revolutionary Science of Biofluorescence*. Cambridge, MA: Belknap Press of Harvard University Press, 2005. Explains further details on the lives of scientists studying living light, most especially Osamu Shimomura. Focuses on the discovery of GFP and its many uses.

Zimmer, Marc. *Glowing Genes: A Revolution in Biotechnology*. Amherst, NY: Prometheus Books, 2005. Describes new research on the many fascinating uses for GFP and other fluorescent proteins.

Fun with Photoluminescence

Glow in the Dark: Ocean Creatures. Discovery Kids. DK Publishing, 2003. Glow-in-the-dark stickers of ocean creatures.

Masden, Chris. *Sea Creatures: Glow-in-the-Dark Sticker Book*. Dutton Juvenile, Sticker Edition, 2000. More about ocean life in general, as well as bioluminescent creatures, using glow-in-the-dark stickers.

Web Sites*

Harbor Branch Oceanographic Institute. *www.biolum.org* Great photos of many bioluminescent creatures. Nicely organized, reliable information from experts on how and why creatures make light. Covers bacteria, dinoflagellates, crustaceans, jellies, fish. Also contains information on how bioluminescent ocean creatures are studied.

International Society for Bioluminescence and Chemiluminescence. *www.unibo.it/isbc* Includes information about the Bologna Stone.

Montana State University–Bozeman Bioglyphs Project. *www.erc.montana.edu/Bioglyphs* View all the artwork from two exhibitions of glowing bacteria at the Montana State University.

Tufts University. *ase.tufts.edu/biology/firefly/index.html* Some complicated explanations, but some great photos and diagrams of fireflies. Includes a description of how they can turn their flashes on and off using nitric oxide.

University of California, Santa Barbara. *www.lifesci.ucsb.edu/biolum* The Bioluminescence Web Page A treasure chest of expert explanations, illustrations, wonderful photos, and movies about bioluminescence and the marine creatures that have it. Many cool extras appear when you click on the links in the text. In the photo section, choose a photo of an ocean creature to learn more about it.

To Purchase Dinoflagellates for Science Projects

Carolina Biological Supply Company. *www2.carolina.com*
Sunnyside Sea Farms. *www.seafarms.com*

*Active at the time of publication

Glossary

ATP (adenosine triphosphate) a chemical that works as an energy transfer system in living cells

bathysphere a globe-shaped diving device that is lowered into the ocean and carries scientists studying ocean life

bioluminescence cool light produced by a chemical reaction inside a living organism

catalyst a substance needed for a chemical reaction to take place that is neither changed nor used up in the reaction

chemical reaction the combination of two or more chemicals to form a new substance

chemiluminescence light at low temperatures produced by a chemical reaction

dinoflagellate single-celled organism with characteristics of plants and animals. Most dinoflagellates float on the ocean and produce their own light.

diode an electric part that allows electricity to flow in only one direction

DNA (deoxyribonucleic acid) substance in the nucleus of a cell that carries information for heredity in the form of genes

electron a small particle that orbits the nucleus (center) of an atom

enzyme a substance found in living cells that promotes chemical reactions

fluorescence another name for photoluminescence

fluorescent protein a protein that gives off cool light

gene the unit of heredity that passes on traits from one generation to the next

GFP (green fluorescent protein) found in jellyfish, it produces green light when blue light or ultraviolet light is shone on it

LED (light-emitting diode) an electronic chip, or diode, designed to emit light, which is covered by a plastic bulb

luc **gene** a gene that causes a firefly to produce luminescence

luciferase the enzyme that helps luciferin make cold light in bioluminescent organisms

luciferin the chemical needed to make cold light in bioluminescent organisms

luminescence light produced with little or no heat

lux **gene system** genes that cause luminescence in bacteria

OLED (organic light-emitting diode) an LED that uses substances like GFP from living organisms to produce light

phosphor a material that gives off cool light when its electrons are excited

photocyte a special light-producing cell in photophores of bioluminescent creatures

photoluminescence luminescence (cool light) produced by an outside light source acting on a phosphor

photophore a special light organ in a bioluminescent creature

recombinant DNA combined DNA of two different organisms

synthesize to make something by combining all its parts

Index (Page numbers in *italics* refer to captions.)

Abraliopsis (squid), *24*, 24–25, *25*

Aequorea victoria. See jellyfish

alchemy, 8–9

anglerfish, 26–27, *27*

Applegate, Bruce, *12*

atoms, 7–8

ATP (adenosine triphosphate), 28–29, 46

bacteria, 12–15, 21, 26, 29, 32–33, 35–36, 40

Barton, Otis, 23

bathysphere, 23, 46

Beebe, William, 22–23, 27

beetles, 16, 18, *18*, 21, 30

Benaron, David, 36

bioluminescence, 5, 10–14, 19–23, 26–29, 31, 36–37, 39, 46

Bologna Stone, 7–9, *8*, 10

Boyle, Robert, 10–14, 19

Bright, Nathan, *12*

Bryan, Bruce, 37

burglar alarm, 21

calcium, 37

cancer, 36–37, 39

Casciarolo, Vincenzo, 8–11

catalyst, 29, 46

Chaenophryne longiceps (anglerfish), *27*

Chalfie, Martin, 39

chemical reactions, 5, 10, 19, 28–29, 46

chemicals, 5, 19, 21–22, 29, 39–40

chemiluminescence, 5, 36, 41, 46

cloning, 32–33, 40–41

Contag, Christopher, 36

Contag, Pamela, 36

cucujo, 18, *18*

Cypridina, 21

dinoflagellates, 20–21, 46

diode, 41, 46. *See also* LEDs; OLEDs

DNA, 32–34, *34*, 36, 39, 46. *See also* recombinant DNA

dragonfish, 26, *26*

DsRed, 40, *40*

Dubois, Raphael, 16, 19

electricity, 7–8, 41–42, 44

electrons, 7–10, 42, 46

energy, 7–8, 10, 28, 41–42, 44

enzyme, 19, 28, 31, 46

filament, *6*, 7, 42

Finley, Gene, 37

fire beetle (*Pyrophorus*), 16, 18, *18*, 21

fireflies, 5, 8–9, 18, 21–22, 27–31, 37, 41

   chemicals of, 29, 31

   codes of, 30–31

flashlight fish, 12–13, 27

fluorescence, 10, 46

fluorescent proteins, 40, 46. *See also* GFP

fox fire, 16–17

fungi, 16–17, 19

GFP (green fluorescent protein), 37–41, 43, 46

glow-in-the-dark objects, 5, 8–10, 37–38

glow sticks. *See* light sticks

Harvey, E. Newton, 19–23, 27–28

hatchet fish, 27

incandescence, 7, 43

jellyfish, 16, 21–22, 27, 36–41, 43
    Aequorea victoria, *38*, 38–39
    chemicals of, 37, 39

Lampyridae, 30
lantern fish, 25
Lapis solaris, 9
LEDs (light-emitting diodes), 41–44, 46
light bulbs, 7–8, 14, 43–44
light organs. *See* photophores
light-producing structures, 27
    See also photocytes
light sticks, 5
luc genes, 32, 35–36, 46
luciferase, 19, 22, 28, 31–32, 37, 39–41, 46
luciferin, 19, 22, 28, 31–32, 35, 37, 39–41, 46
Lukyanov, Sergey, 40
luminescence, 5, 8–9, *38*, 46
    See also bioluminescence; chemiluminescence;
    photoluminescence
lux genes, *33*, 35–36, 46

magnesium, 29
mating, 13, 18, 25–26, 30
Matz, Mikhail, 40
McElroy, William, 27–30, 32, 37
mice, 36, *39*
Monte Paderno, 9
mushroom, 11, 16–17, *17*

Nakamura, Shuji, 43
N-type silicon, 42

OLEDs (organic light-emitting diodes), 43, 46
ostracods, 21–22, *22*

oxygen, 12–13, 19, 28, 37

phosphors, 9, 43, 46
photocytes, 31, 46
photoluminescence, 10, 46
photophores (light organs), *24*, 24–25, 31, 46
    See also light-producing structures
Prasher, Douglas, 39
predators, 21, 25, 31
prey, 25
Prolume, 37, 39
P-type silicon, 42
Pyrophorus. See fire beetle

recombinant DNA, 32–33, 35–36, 40, 46

semiconductor, 42
Shimomura, Osamu, 39
squid, *24*, 24–25, 27

Vargula hilgendorfii (Cypridina). See ostracods